RAIN ANGEL

CHRIS TUTTON

AVALANCHE BOOKS

Published in Great Britain by Avalanche Books, England.

British Library Cataloguing in Publication Data. A catalogue record for this book is available from the British Library.

Printed in Great Britain by SRP, England.

ISBN 1 874392 08 0

For dearest Roo with endless love and gratitude

and

for Sapphie and Ray with love and sorrow

Contents

DAFFODILS

Hawthorn fringed this
                    Scrub
A nursery once
We coursed contours of spiked
                    Green
Circumventing flowerbeds
In scuffed shoes

Golden brocade spanned this
                    Hill
A spring of daffodils seeped
And we ran until blooms
                    Became
Empty spaces
Framed by footprints.

(for Ray Tutton 1960-2001)

ECHO OF DESIRE

I bit my lip
When you left,
An untold kiss
Raisined on the vine.

DRYADS

In autumn perished
Fruitless withered orchard
Leaves fall
Ochre wings
Ford the inlet
Lace a string
Of bleeding pearls

BESIDE YEWS

I have spent
All afternoon
Sitting beside you
Listening to flies
Buzz between us
Like chainsaws.

FAVOURITE STREET

Back on favourite street
Don't need a crutch,
Walking slowly in a
Milling crowd
Almost disguises
My limp.

THE BRIAR REAPER

In the broken heart of your
Grieving garden sunlit
Mahonia sweet
Aired by a changing tide
You tread softly in the
Shallow of your reflection
Planting thorns for roses.

THE THUNDER BEARER

Sweat upon sweat
From day to
Strolling homeward over
Varicose veins of
Purple hill's
Night furrowed brow
Blood spill sky
Drips like
Brushes on tympani
Heather underfoot
Counterpoint
Sporting choruses of
Contemplation
And two black dogs
In my satchel
Both hungry.

THE ABSENCE OF WONDER

Sunlight plays upon the lake
Disappears beneath the surface
A ripple, a few air bubbles
Then nothing.

THE RAIN MAKER

Sometimes
Beneath
Watery skies
There are
Days
When
All lovers
Have parted.

THE KISS

I want to live
Long enough to
Enjoy my death
To offer it the
Hospitality of a
Convivial host
To embrace it tenderly
Like a woman I
Have always loved.

CHROMATIC CONFLICT

Your sombre colour
Matched my mood
But then my mood changed
And we clashed badly.

BEYOND THE EDGE OF REASON

We drove
All through
The night
From familiarity
To contempt
Not even
Stopping for
The red lights.

AFFECTED

It's funny, thought Nigel, as he
Reflected on the passing of
A dizzy rush of summers, how,
In the flower of my youth
I became allergic to pollen.

PROJECTION WHEEL DISASTER

I just can't get this image
Out of my head,
Sighed Norma,
Bleeding profusely.

THE SHADOW

The small boy looked behind him and noticed
there was darkness.
'There is something dark behind me, father,'
he exclaimed in some surprise.
'It is your shadow,' replied the old man, tenderly.
'Can it harm me?' asked the small boy anxiously.
The old man watched smiling as the small boy
attempted to disengage himself from his
unyielding appendage.
'That will depend,' the old man advised after a
few moments of quiet amusement,
'on where you allow it to fall.'

RESTRICTED PERSPECTIVE

There were times when
We felt we had succeeded
Other times we thought we had failed
Occasionally we could not be sure
Precisely how we had fared.
Mostly we concluded
That the possible was an
Ill determined area which
Could not be charted accurately.

DENOUEMENT

I am sick of
These props I have
Maintained so meticulously,
Sighed Nigel,
Discarding a script.
I have acted out
My life to critics
Who were interested
In nothing but
Free drinks during
The interval.

ON THE EIGHTH DAY

I found God
Dying in a
Doorway on
Saint Anthony Street,
Call an ambulance
Call a doctor
Call a priest.
He took my
Hand tamely and
In a thin voice asked:
'My son, can you save me?'
I didn't say anything
Right away;
I just kind of
Looked at him
For a moment,
Confused.

THE UNANSWERED CALL

Silently, inexorably,
Black dogs lost on the
Dark side of night
We lose scent of the chase
In torched fields where we
Leave each other wandering.

MIDWINTER

You caught me
Staring into the past
An old man
Hankering after
A kiss.

THE CURTAIN

He contrived to save
His best morning for last
Button holed the myrtle
Kissed the blushing bride
Drew a curtain on the
Small boy
Lifting tin sheets
Trying to catch
Slow-worms in the brickfields.

DAWN CHORUS

On these
Quiet mornings
I like to sit
In an open field
Listening to
Blackbirds pecking
Songs from my flesh.

FROM LANTERN WINDOWS

I still see you
In late spring
Beneath
Cornelion cherries
Holding
The ivy.

THE FALL OF TROY

Before it became dark we watched rabbits
Trickle down the hillside like spring water
Wild geese fleck mandarin suns
Spilling amber into the chenille of our shadow.
Before it became dark we fashioned
Moments into memories
Which would become
Too difficult to hold.
Before it became dark we
Touched each other gently
When we walked
Arm in arm like
Barge mules inching the towpath.

HALCYON MORNING

Those were the days
When we could
Sit on the
Crenellated railway bridge
High above the tracks
Taking in the sun and
Not even thinking
Of jumping.

POSSOM RISING

'Who the hell do I think I'm kidding?'
Sighed Nigel,
Kicking himself sharply in
A sensitive moment.
'It is becoming increasingly obvious
That my gift for playing dead
Has been completely wasted
On this life.'

THE IDIOT

When I was
Younger I
Used to
Play the idiot.
Now that I
Am older
I don't need
To play
Quite so hard.

TUIST REPLY

You speak my words
So beautifully
You make me wish
That I had thought of them.

SYMPHONY OF SIGHS

I dreamed I looked out upon
A sea of drowning angels,
Thought Martha, as she
Crocheted a pupil for a
Stained glass iris,
But when I looked more closely
I could see that they were
Not drowning at all;
They were merely
Gasping for air.

AN ANTICIPATED LAPSE

The day draughts
Its portrait
On my memory
Like waves
Over sand.

THE DINNER PARTY

I arose without speaking, while many of the specially
assembled delegation of distinguished arachnids were
spinning and already suspending glistening wisps of
platitude above my anticipated departure like tomb tinsel.
I, of course, without intending an encore, had already died
enough times to last a lifetime by the time I was forcibly
delivered stillborn into the world at the age of forty. And
although my leaden exit was hardly surprise enough to have
batted even the most gullible insect's eyelid, I excused
myself to my conscience with the conviction that I could
not be sure I had ever actually been there. Like my name,
I felt I had only previously existed as a reference to
something more abstruse.
The applause, the abrasive, percussive, cacophonic ensemble
rustling of hirsute forelegs at the foot of my ensuing eulogy
staggered awkwardly on like a drunken song that nobody
seemed quite able to remember, until someone interrupted a
less than rousing chorus by coughing loudly to signal that
sufficient discomfort had been endured by all as a tribute to
my departure, and that dinner was about to be served on a
new bed of shingle.

ESCULAPIAN RETREAT

Where were the angels
When we needed them?
At the station you
Leaving without speaking
Me watching you pull
Away into the distance
Without even
Raising an arm.

OCEAN OF SORROW

Lillian

We passed like
Two ships
In the night
Running aground on
Different beaches.

Isobel

We passed like
Two ships in
Broad daylight
Blinded by the sun
Each not noticing
That the other
Was sinking.

Katriona

We did not
Pass at
Any time
More like
Lighthouses than
Ships overlooking
A vast stretch of
Sea that
Neither of us
Could cross.

THE SEED TINDER

We were drawn to the long days like
Supplicants eager to be warm
Chasing Loggerheads in
Leeched brooks barefoot
Kingfishers on the wing
Hurrying crickets home to
Discover there were
Ghosts in these summers that
Would not let us gather seasons easily.

PORTRAIT IN FADING COLOURS

I painted you
Playful in bower shadow
Where whistling jacks grow
Arboured by dusk.
You beckoned me
Reclining clover veiled like
An uncertain bride
From the time when we were
Younger and watched
Lumpsuckers skim the millpond.

EPILOGUE

Seasons have reduced you to winter
Dark flameless ringed
Like ancient timber
Sad eyed
Cradling my smile
As if it were
Your own child.

THE ADORNMENT

I have learned to
Pluck the pearl
From the open shell
Of every new day,
Sighed Martha,
Stringing a
Necklace of optimism
Too delicate to wear.

DELUGE

There is a man in here
Lying in a hollow
Looking out at the rain
Waiting to sleep.

THE APPRENTICE

I want to learn to
Paint from the heart,
Sighed Nigel,
Opening a vein.

THE GHOST DANCE

He stood on the promontory
Torn from the ankle
Knee deep in frost
Above ebb tide.
They heard him fracture
A precarious silence
In which the uncomfortable
Had been denied.
Some thought he was
Howling at the moon
But he wasn't.
He hadn't even
Noticed the moon.

A SPRIG OF ROSEMARY

The old woman
Began to snow
Closing her eyes
Slowly as the
Flakes fell
Remembering
A name.

FALTERING TENDER

I have

cultivated the music of

angels

in the fullness

of silence

thought Martha,

nervously

attempting to sing without

breaking

the moment.

THE GHOST OF EVERYTHING

We were
Warriors
When the nights
Were short
Youthful
Immortal
Armed with
Kisses and sighs
Armed with
Kisses and sighs
Bloodied blissful in
Fields of stone
Older than
We became.

THE SHIVER

In winter I
Feel like a
Stranger
Retracing footprints
I cannot remember
Leaving.

TRUMPET OF MORNING

Unthinking
Unfeeling
I return to
Your beach
Like flotsam
Blown in on
The lee.

SUNSET INCURSION

There you stand
Shrouded in
Departure lounge
Anticipation of
A flight to
Unbreachable borders
Waving the handkerchief
Holding back
Untellable goodbyes.

AMARANTH WINDOW

Sometimes I see you
In strangers who
Do not look back.

THE CRUCIFIXION

Pain is not a thing I am
Comfortable with, thought
Nigel, as he nailed his
Ankle to the trunk
Of a beech tree,
But I would rather
Do something useful
Than feel I have
Completely wasted yet
Another precious day.

THE MATINEE IDOL

Wellington had missed Christmas by six weeks. He purred to himself softly but he was no cat. Stroking the window with a longing to be outside, he fixed a grin on his reflection before dropping it like a tear and, retreating into the quiet calm of a comforting daydream, imagined his wrists to be bleeding.

HARMONY OF OPPOSITES

We spent the evening
Admiring each others suggestions
Trading signals that
Neither of us was sure of.

EXODUS

We were
Beach born
Hatchlings
Skeltering from
The hourglass
To the sea.

THE WEIGH IN

He looked life
In the eye but
Life stared him down;
You could tell
Right away that
It was never
Going to be
An evenly matched
Encounter.

APATHETIC ANGUISH

There was always more or less
To want from my life,
Sighed Nigel, but
My heart was never in it;
I could happily have been
The architect of my own downfall
Had I not been too idle to secure
The appropriate planning permission.

BAD COMPANY

I'd like to be
Alone with my thoughts,
Sighed Martha,
But I can't help thinking
That I'd be safer
With a chaperone.

HEADBANGING

Night clubbing can
Kill you;
Ask any
Seal pup.

ON THE PRECIPICE OF KNOWLEDGE

Like ornamental ducks we sat
Perched on the silver bridge wondering
Why it was called silver
When it was made of wood.
We sat waiting for the day to fall
Gasping blue like an asthmatic thief
Shot in the back by a brass moon rising
And then we ambled home along
The dust track thinking of
Other things that confused us.

SEVEN SHADES OF DOUBT

It is all the colours
I varnished you
Which have faded
In the sun that
I stood you in to
See you clearer.

UMBRA

I am afraid
Of the night
Tormented
By the dark
Hanged
By the rope
I paint with
My left hand.

REPROACHMENT

Not even a force ten gale
Could blow as many
Opportunities as I have,
Thought Nigel,
Regretting the opportunity
He had not taken
To remove himself
From a force ten gale.

BROKEN GROUND

We were conscientious objectors
Unprepared to take up arms
Or allegiances
Helpless, tear stained
Running upstairs to escape
The slaughter of our innocence
Fingering our ears to
Mute the battle cries
We were the peacemakers
The dispossessed, the war orphans
Slipping round the back of the
Dance hall on Saturday night
Looking for affection like it had been
Lost there in the darkness.

A QUESTION OF UNCERTAINTY

Everything is so confusing
When you are young
Like whether you should feel
Guilty or envious when you
Walk past the orphanage.

THE IMAGE

God watched his
Fame disappear beneath
A cloud of game shows.
'I am the anti-Christ,'
He announced
One day,
Hoping to grab
The headlines.

DOPPLEGANGER

I seem to be acting
Strangely out of character
Thought Nigel,
Secretly suspecting
Himself of being
Somebody else.

SHOCK OF THE NEW

After I was baptised
I was told that
Jesus had entered me.
I felt distressed
Confused and
Hell bent on vengeance.

THE END OF ALL RAINBOWS

Some days there
Is not a
Cloud in the sky.
Or a sky.

NOCTURNAL CROSSING

I pass my evenings
Whistling in the dark
Like a train
Enroute to
A song.

NEPENTHE THIRST

I held you again tonight
Half light fingers stroked
Memories in your shadow,
Drank a well of your kiss from
The lip of my wineglass
Missed you more than
The dregs of
My last swallow.

INVISIBLE FOOTNOTE

Words became wind
Silence counsel
Touch became feeling
As we fell
Helpless
From ash to ash.

CLOSURE

Harvesting the desolation of unguarded dreams
Slipping footloose on the scree of rumour
Wading littoral in gibbous moon tide turning
From companion of my thoughts
To adversary of my actions
Seeking the one golden
Constant church of daybreak
And a single truth that
Will not tarnish in sunlight.

LEXICON OF LOSS

We spend our lives
Communicating with the dead
Without ever really
Mastering the dialect.

AEONIAN PURSUIT

I have read a
Library of eyes
In search of
The perfect novel.

RAIN ANGEL

A whisp of birdsong
Airborne
A purple sunset kiss
On the
Spire of evening
A weeping
Hollared dirge
A midnight
Choir of yearning
A new dawn
Will not rouse you.

SEPIA ROADS

We can no longer
Brush away tears
Which have etched themselves
Into fleshlines
Nor load the bristle
With the brilliant tones
Of our first embrace
Now that the oaks have grown
And we stand
A little smaller in their shade
Fumbling for
Each other's hand
Over painting
Deeper sepia roads.